This Naughty Book
Belongs To

_____

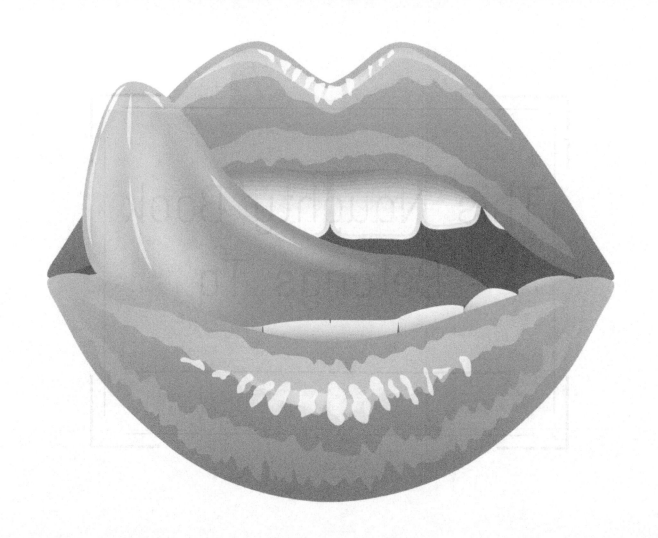

BONUS

Want Free Goodies?!

Email us at

naughtyloversvalentine@gmail.com

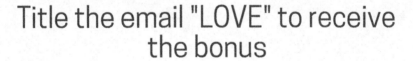

Title the email "LOVE" to receive
the bonus

Enjoy the book!

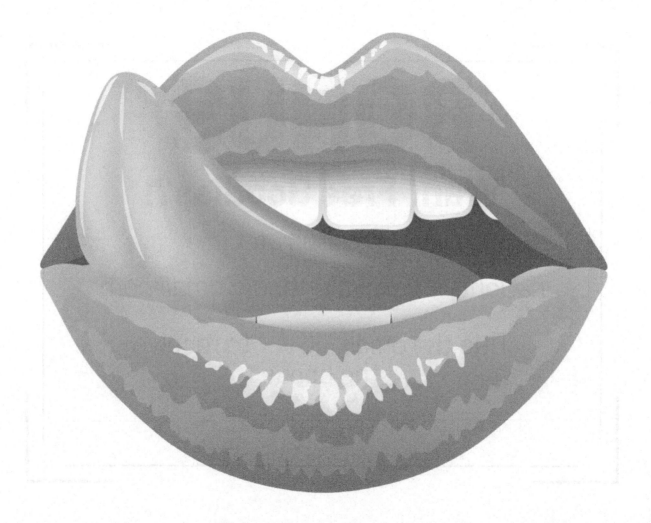

Let's Get Freaky Anywhere But The Bedroom Night

Hotel Night And Only My Favorite Positions

Wake Me Up With Oral Sex

Sexy Lap Dance With A Dress And No Panties

Lunch Quickie

Let's Bathe Together And Have Sex

Quickie In An Elevator

1 Hour Oral Sex

Blindfold Me And Give Me The Best Blowjob Of My Life

Let Me Have An Orgasm On Your Breasts

69 Until I Orgasm

Don't Wear Panties At A Movie Night

Keep The Lights
On And
Masturbate With
Your Fingers
Before I
Penetrate You

Let Me Masturbate And Finish On Any Part Of Your Body

Talk Dirty To Me All Day Long On A Weekday, And When I Arrive Home Don't Say Nothing, Let's Just Have Sex

Ride Me Until I Orgasm...Take Your Time

Put Ice Cream On My Penis And Lick It...Slowly...Take A Pause, Look At My Eyes..And Finish All

Role Play All Night

Let's Watch Porn An Re-Enact My Favorite Positions

Let's Have Sex On A Beach

Let's Have Sex In A Car

Quickie In An Elevator

Let's Make A Homemade Porno

Sex On A Rooftop

Let's Masturbate At The Same Time And Look In Each Other Eyes

Just Use Heels
On The Bed

Let Me Grope You In A Public Place

Let's Go To A Hotel/Motel With A Mirror On The Celling, And Watch Us Having Sex

Let's Get Drunk
At Home And
Have Crazy Sex,
Scream As Loud
As You Can

Quickie In A Club Or Some Public Place

Send Me Nudes While You Are At Your Workplace

Let Me Finger You Under A Restaurant Table

Let's Have Sex
In A Pool

Give Me Oral Sex...While You Masturbate

Let's Have A Threesome...I Choose The Person

Let's Have A Quickie In A Friends/Family House

Give Me A Handjob At The Movies

Plenty Of Lube And Only Anal Sex Night

Sex Call During Lunch At Workplace

Let Me Have An Orgasm In Your Mouth/Face At Least 2 Times In One Night

Give Me A Blowjob...While I'am Watching Sports

Give Me A Blowjob...But Let Me Orgasm In Your Anus

Let Me Have An Orgasm In Your Face

Let Me Have An Orgasm Inside Your Mouth

Do One Of My Crazy Sex Fantasies

Give Me A Blowjob...And Swallow Everything

Tie Me Up...Blow Me Until I Orgasm...Then Blow Me Again...Don't Let Me Rest

When You Are
Giving Me A
Blowjob...Let Me
Slap You Gently
With My Penis

Do Whatever I Want For 30 Minutes

Let Me Finger
Your Anus While
We Are Having
Sex and You Are
In All Fours

Want More?

Check out our collection

Let's Put The Sausage In The Bun
Sex Coupons For Couples

http://getbook.at/SausageInTheBun

Can You Handle It?
Sex Challenge Book For Couples

http://getbook.at/CanYouHandleIt

Sit On My Face And Glaze Me Like A Doughnut
Sex Coupons For Her

http://getbook.at/SitOnMyFace

Make Your Own Coupons

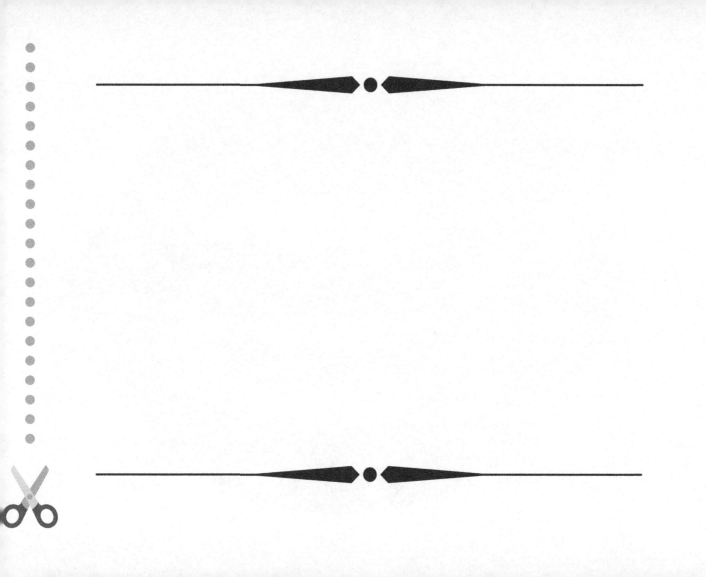

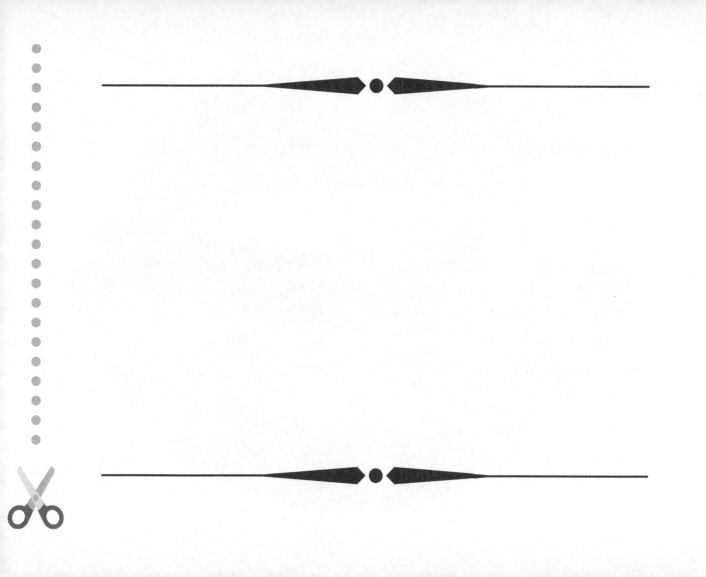

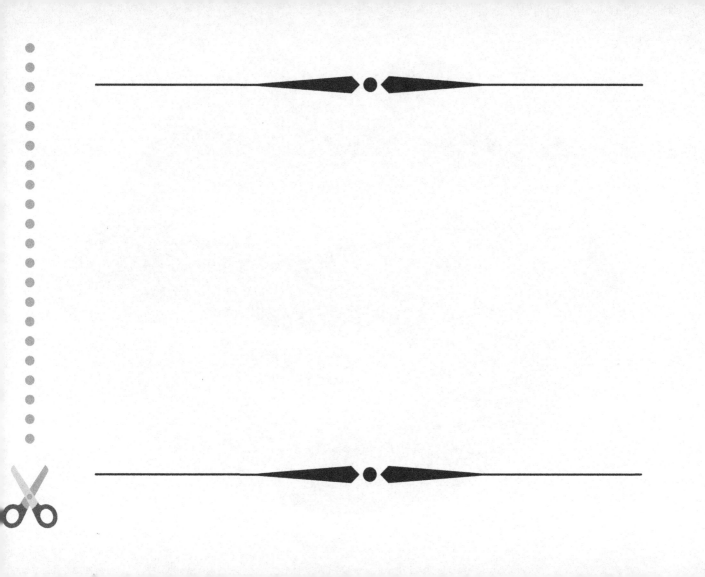

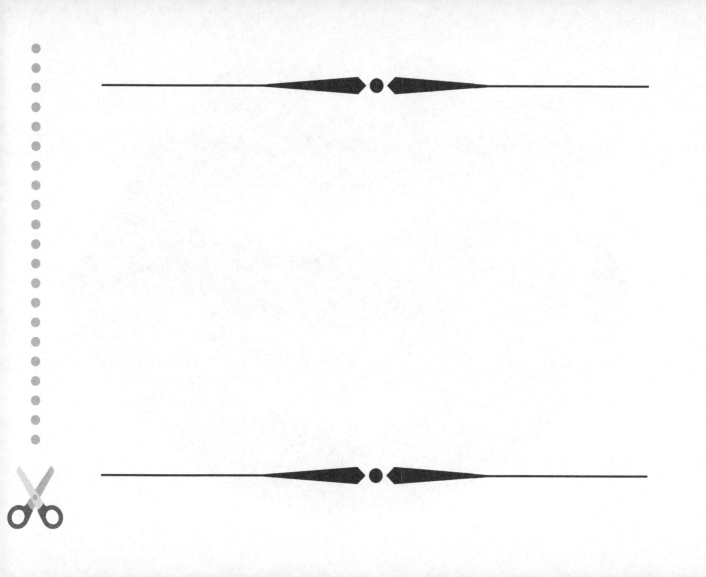

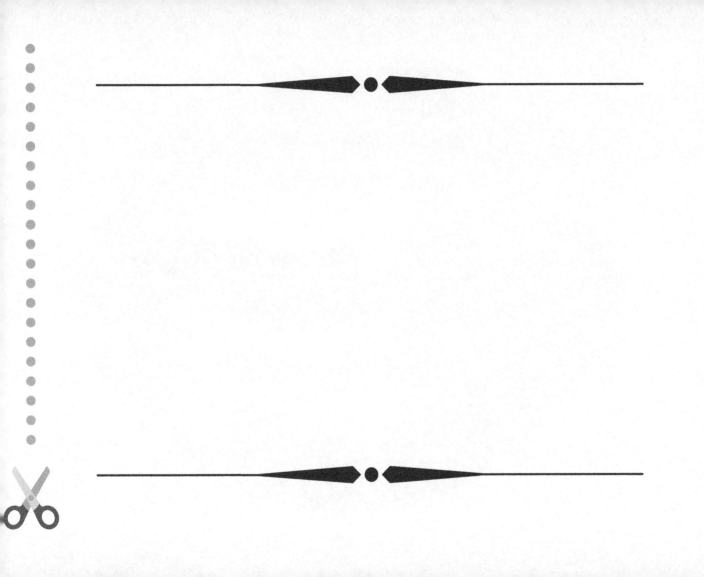

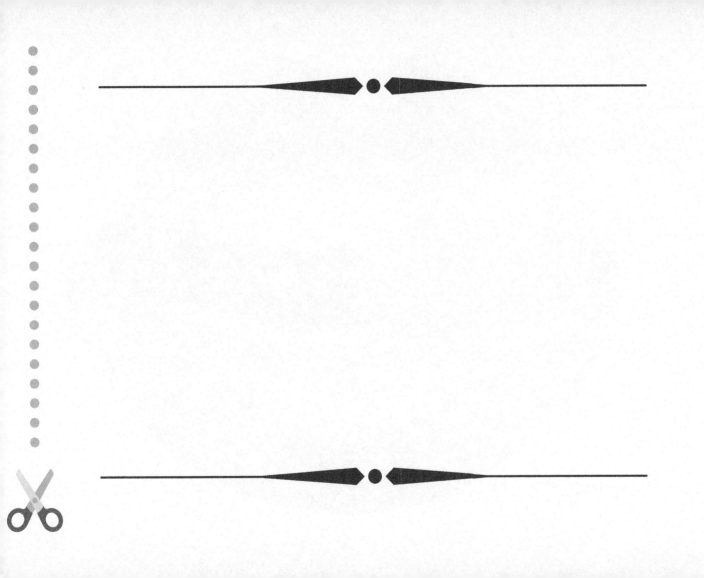

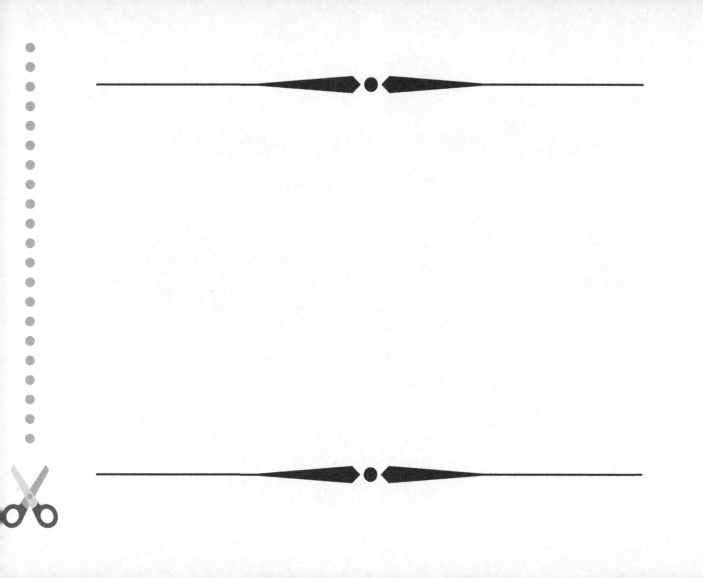

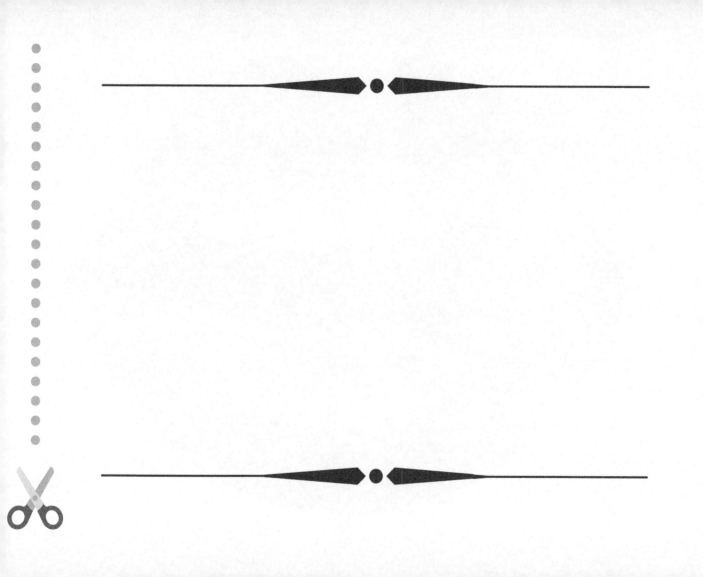

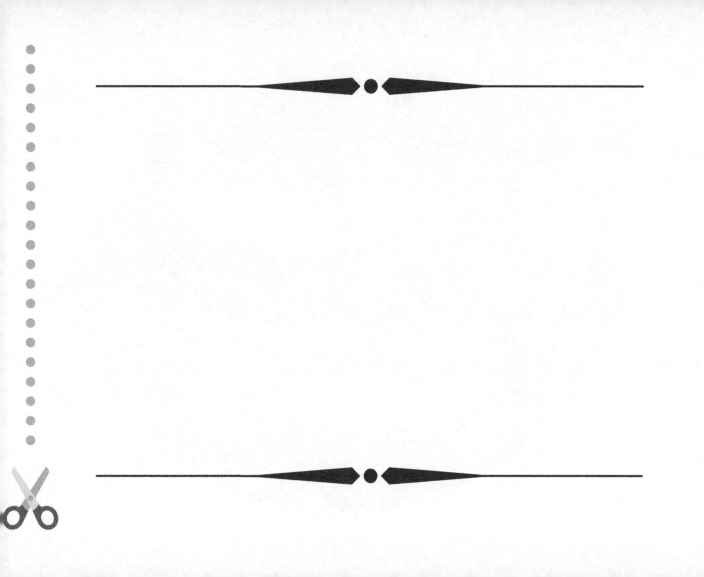

Made in United States
Orlando, FL
16 November 2024

53964269R00070